The MOM Dictionary

drawings by:

Valerie McKeown

A SHOEBOX GREETINGS Book
(A tiny little division of Hallmark)

Andrews and McMeel
A Universal Press Syndicate Company
Kansas City

Other SHOEBOX GREETINGS Books from Andrews and McMeel
(A tiny little division of Hallmark)

Raiders of the Lost Bark!
Workin' Noon to Five
Don't Worry, Be Crabby!

WRITTEN BY: Chris Brethwaite,
Bill Bridgeman, Renee Duvall, Bill Gray,
Allyson Jones, Kevin Kinzer, Mark Oatman,
Scott Oppenheimer, Dee Ann Stewart,
Dan Taylor, Richard Warwick and
Myra Zirkle.

ISBN: 0-8362-1732-2

Library of Congress Catalog Card Number: 93-71013

ABC'S: First three letters of the alphabet, often taught by Mom in song to her child, after which Mom gets the pleasure of hearing the song ten- to fifteen thousand times, with only the last twenty-five or so sung correctly.

ADULTS: Group of people Mom longs to communicate with after several hours of talking in small words about topics like "who touched who first."

AEROBICS: Exercise class where Mom used to have to go in order to burn calories before she had kids to keep up with.

AIRPLANE: What Mom impersonates to get a 1-year-old to eat strained beets.

8

ALIEN: What Mom would suspect had invaded her house if she spotted a child-sized creature cleaning up after itself.

APPLE: Nutritious lunchtime dessert which kids trade for cupcakes.

BABY: 1) Dad, when he gets a cold. 2) Mom's youngest child, even if he's 42.

BATHROOM: A room used by the entire family, believed by all except Mom to be self-cleaning.

BECAUSE: Mom's reason for having kids do things which can't be explained logically.

BED AND BREAKFAST: Two things the kids will never make for themselves.

BEETS: What a baby is sure to spit up if Mom is wearing a white blouse.

BLUE: Color Mom talks until she is "in the face."

CANDY: Snack items that Moms try in vain to make sound less tempting than slices of apple or little celeries with peanut butter on them.

мммм

CARPET: Expensive floor covering used to catch spills and clean mud off shoes.

CAR POOL: Complicated system of transportation where Mom always winds up going the furthest with the biggest bunch of kids who have had the most sugar.

CHINA: Legendary nation reportedly populated by children who love leftover vegetables.

COOK: 1) Act of preparing food for consumption. 2) Mom's other name.

COUCH POTATO: What Mom finds under the sofa cushions after the kids eat dinner.

DATE: Infrequent outings with Dad where Mom can enjoy worrying about the kids in different settings.

DRINKING GLASS: Any carton or bottle left open in the refrigerator.

DUST: Insidious interloping particles of evil that turn a home into a battle zone.

DUST RAGS: See "Dad's Underwear."

EAR: A place where kids store dirt.

EAT: What kids do between meals, but not at them.

EMPTY NEST: See "Wishful Thinking."

ENERGY: Element of vitality
kids always have an oversupply
of until asked to do something.

"EXCUSE ME": One of Mom's favorite phrases, reportedly used in past times by children.

EYE: The highly susceptible optic nerve which, according to Mom, can be "put out" by anything from a suction-cup arrow to a carelessly handled butter knife.

FABLE: A story by a teenager arriving home after curfew.

FOOD: The response Mom usually gives in answer to the question "What's for dinner tonight?" See "Sarcasm."

FOOTBALL GAME: What Mom attends on Friday nights in below-zero weather to watch her kid on the bench for two hours.

FROZEN: 1) A type of food. 2) How hell will be when Mom lets her daughter date a guy with a motorcycle.

GARBAGE: A collection of refuse items, the taking out of which Mom assigns to a different family member each week, then winds up doing herself.

GENIUSES: Amazingly, all of Mom's kids.

GRAVITY: Force of nature that holds kids' clothing to the bedroom floor.

GROCERY CART: Mobile storage device invented for shopping ease which holds items Mom is completely unaware the kids have snuck in until she reaches the checkout line.

GUM: Adhesive for the hair.

HAMPER: A wicker container with a lid, usually surrounded by, but not containing, dirty clothing.

HANDI-WIPES: Pants, shirtsleeves, drapes, etc.

HANDS: Body appendages which must be scrubbed raw with volcanic soap and sterilized in boiling water immediately prior to consumption of the evening meal.

HINDSIGHT: What Mom experiences from changing too many diapers.

HOMEMADE BREAD: An object of fiction like the Fountain of Youth and the Golden Fleece.

ICE: Cubes of frozen water which would be found in small plastic trays if kids or husbands ever filled the darn things instead of putting them back in the freezer empty.

ICKY: A child's word to describe a new recipe.

IMITATE: What one child will do to another in an attempt to drive them, and Mom, to the brink of insanity.

INSIDE: That place that will suddenly look attractive to kids once Mom has spent half an hour getting them ready to go outside.

"I SAID SO": Reason enough,
according to Mom.

JEANS: Clothing which, according to kids, is appropriate for just about any occasion, including church and funerals.

"JEEEEEEZ!": Slang for "Gee Mom, isn't there anything else you can do to embarrass me in front of my friends?"

JOYRIDE: Going somewhere without the kids.

JUNK: Dad's stuff.

KEEP: What a mom does with any toy a kid plays with in church.

"KEEP IT DOWN TO A DULL ROAR": Expression Mom thinks is clever, but kids don't understand and therefore ignore.

KETCHUP: The sea of tomato-based goop kids use to drown the dish that Mom spent hours cooking and years of perfecting to get the seasoning just right.

KISS: Mom medicine.

KITE: A flying device invented to make parents look silly.

KLUTZ: A term never used to describe one of Mom's kids. Instead, it's an "awkward age he's going through."

LAKE: Large body of water into which a kid will jump should his friends do so.

LEMONADE STAND: Complicated business venture where Mom buys powdered mix, sugar, lemons and paper cups, and sets up a table, chairs, pitchers and ice for kids who sit there for three to six minutes and net a profit of 15 cents.

LIE: An "exaggeration" Mom uses to transform her child's papier-mâché volcano science project into a Nobel Prize-winning experiment and a full-ride scholarship to Harvard.

LOSERS: See "Kids' Friends."

48

MAKEUP: Lipstick, eyeliner, blush, etc., which ironically make Mom look better while making her young daughter look "like a tramp."

MAYBE: No

can I have a skateboard like Joe's for my birthday?

Maybe

MICROWAVE: Mom's little gift from heaven.

MIDDLE NAME:
Something your
parents gave you
when you were born,
so your mom could
use it when she
was really mad.

MILK: A healthful beverage which kids will gladly drink once it's turned into junk food by the addition of sugar and cocoa.

"MOMMMM!": The cry of a child on another floor who wants something.

MUSH: 1) What a kid loves to do with a plateful of food. 2) Main element of Mom's favorite movies.

NAILS: A hard covering on the end of the finger, which Mom can never have a full set of due to pitching batting practice, opening stubborn modeling clay lids and removing heat ducts to retrieve army men or doll clothing.

NO: Apparently, the single most difficult word for children to understand.

NOISE: How Mom refers to any music her kids like.

OATMEAL: Food item which "sticks to kids' ribs." It also sticks to tablecloths, floors, chairs and amazingly, ceilings.

OFFICIAL: The person who is either an eagle eye or blind as a bat, depending on how he makes the call for your child.

OCEAN: What the bathroom floor looks like after bath night for kids, assorted pets, two or three full-sized towels and several dozen toy boats, cars and animals.

OPEN: The position of children's mouths when they eat in front of company.

OVERSTUFFED RECLINER:
Mom's nickname for Dad.

PENITENTIARY: Where children who don't eat their vegetables or clean their rooms eventually end up, according to Mom.

PETS: Small, furry creatures which follow kids home so Mom will have someone to clean up after.

PIANO: A large, expensive musical instrument which, after thousands of dollars worth of lessons and constant harping by Mom, kids will refuse to play in front of company.

PURSE: A handbag in which Mom carries the checkbook and keys she can never find because they're buried under tissues, gum wrappers, a plastic container full of cereal, toys from a fast-food restaurant, a teddy bear, a football, wallpaper samples, a grocery list and several outdated coupons.

QUIET: A state of household serenity which occurs before the birth of the first child and occurs again after the last child has left for college.

QUILT: The 150-year-old bed covering your child "decorated" with a permanent marker.

QUINTS: Mom's recurring nightmare.

QUIZ: What Mom gives to a child who's been on a date.

QUESTIONS: What children ask Mom when she's on the phone.

QUICHE: Mom's diabolical plot to sneak cheese, milk and vegetables into pie.

RABBIT: Type of costume a kid informs Mom he needs for the school Easter pageant the following day.

RADISHES: Right. That'll be the day.

RAINCOAT: Article of clothing Mom bought to keep a child dry and warm, rendered ineffective because it's in the bottom of a locker stuffed in a book bag, or because the child refuses to wear "that geeky thing."

REFRIGERATOR: Combination art gallery and air-conditioner for the kitchen.

ROOM MOTHER: A position of great honor and responsibility bestowed on a mom who inadvertently misses a PTA meeting.

SCHOOL PLAY: Sadistic ritual in which adults derive pleasure from watching offspring stumble through coarse reenactments of famous historic events.

SCREAMING: Home P.A. system.

SNOWSUITS: Warm, padded outer garments that, when completely zipped and snapped perform two important functions: Protecting children from the cold and reminding them that they have to go to the bathroom.

SOAP: A cleaning agent Mom puts on the washbasin on the off chance one of her kids will accidentally grab it while reaching for the towel.

SOMEDAY: That point in time when you'll have your own kids, and every irritating thing Mom has said or done will suddenly become completely clear to you.

SPIT: All-purpose cleaning fluid especially good on kids' faces.

SPOILED ROTTEN: What the kids become after as little as 15 minutes with Grandma.

STRONG-WILLED: Mom's polite term for somebody else's bratty kids.

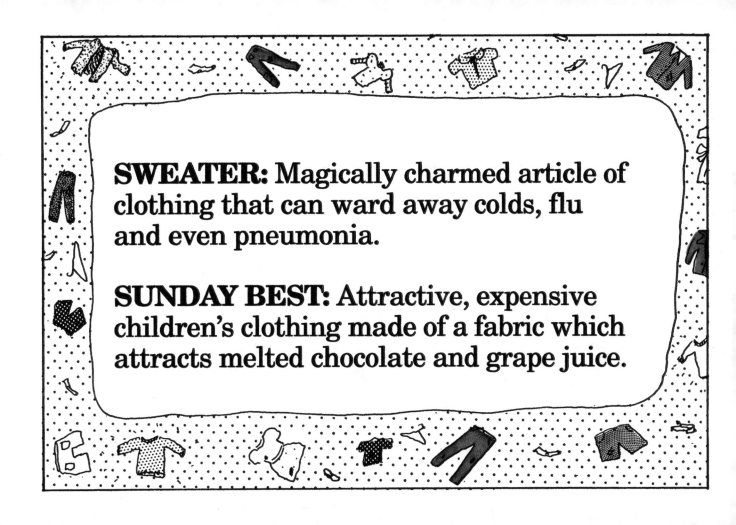

SWEATER: Magically charmed article of clothing that can ward away colds, flu and even pneumonia.

SUNDAY BEST: Attractive, expensive children's clothing made of a fabric which attracts melted chocolate and grape juice.

TEACHER CONFERENCE: A meeting between Mom and that person who has yet to understand her child's "special needs."

TERRIBLE TWO'S: Having both kids at home all summer.

"THAT WAY": How kids shouldn't look at moms if they know what's good for them.

TOWELS: See "Floor Coverings."

TOY BOX: See "Stairs."

TUMBLING: Why all the furniture is pushed against the wall and the lamp is broken.

TRAMP: A woman with two kids and no stretch marks.

TROUBLE: Area of nonspecific space a child is always sure to be in.

UH...UM...: The types of sounds children utter while making up the answer to the "What happened here?" question.

UMPTEENTH: Highly conservative estimate of the number of times Mom must instruct her offspring to do something before it actually gets done.

UNDERWEAR: An article of clothing, the cleanliness of which ensures the wearer will never have an accident.

UTOPIA: See "Bubble Bath."

VACATION: Where you take the family to get away from it all, only to find it there too.

VANILLA: The flavor left for Mom in the Neapolitan ice cream.

VEGETABLES: Health food for the dog.

VCR: Audio-visual device that allows Mom to see movies at home six months after their release because for 10 years she doesn't step foot inside a theater unless it's to see something animated.

VITAMINS: Tiny facsimiles of cave people Mom forces you to swallow each morning as part of her sinister plot to have you grow up to be "just like Daddy."

WALLS: Complete set of drawing paper for kids that comes with every room.

WASHING MACHINE: Household appliance used to clean blue jeans, permanent ink markers, loose change, homework, tissues and wads of gum.

WEAPON: Any normal household item within a child's reach.

"WHEN YOUR FATHER GETS HOME": Standard measurement of time between crime and punishment.

WHEN YOU'RE OLDER: When your Mom will tell you all the stuff she's too embarrassed to tell you now.

WISECRACK: Remark made by kids just loud enough to cause snickering by their peers, but too low for Mom to hear.

XOXOXO: Mom salutation guaranteed to make the already embarrassing note in a kid's lunch box even more mortifying.

XYLOPHONE: Small toy musical instrument often given as gifts to children who show their appreciation by playing the stupid thing constantly over and over all day long! See also "Drums."

YARD SALE: Heart-wrenching emotional process wherein Mom plans to sell kids' outdated toys and clothing that she decides at the last minute are treasured mementos she can't bear to part with.

"YIPPEE!": What Mom would jump up and shout if the school year was changed to 12 months. See "Yahoo!"

YUK!: A child's response to any food that isn't hamburgers or pizza.

ZILLION: Amount of times Mom must have gone to the supermarket already this week.

ZUCCHINI: Vegetable which can be baked, boiled, fried or steamed before kids refuse to eat it.